Barbara
all good wishes
Gladys Mary,
Aug. 03

Leafburners

BY GLADYS MARY COLES

Poetry

THE SOUNDING CIRCLE
SINERVA AND OTHER POEMS
THE SNOW BIRD SEQUENCE
STOAT, IN WINTER
LIVERPOOL FOLIO
STUDIES IN STONE

Biography and Criticism

THE FLOWER OF LIGHT: A BIOGRAPHY OF MARY WEBB
Introductions to Mary Webb's novels GONE TO EARTH and
PRECIOUS BANE
Introduction to Mary Webb's essays THE SPRING OF JOY

As Editor

SELECTED POEMS OF MARY WEBB
MARY WEBB: COLLECTED PROSE AND POEMS

GLADYS MARY COLES

Gladys Mary Coles (signature)

Leafburners

DUCKWORTH

First published in 1986 by
Gerald Duckworth & Co. Ltd.
The Old Piano Factory
43 Gloucester Crescent
London NW1

© 1986 by Gladys Mary Coles

All rights reserved. No part of this publication
may be reproduced, stored in a retrieval system, or
transmitted, in any form or by any means, electronic,
mechanical, photocopying, recording or otherwise, without
the prior permission of the publisher.

ISBN 0 7156 2139 4 (cased)
0 7156 2140 8 (paperback)

British Library Cataloguing in Publication Data

Coles, Gladys Mary
   Leafburners, new and selected poems
   I. Title
   821'.914   PR6053.042/

   ISBN 0-7156-2139-4
   ISBN 0-7156-2140-8 Pbk

Typeset in 10/12pt English Times

Printed and bound in Great Britain by
Redverse Limited
Harlescott, Shrewsbury

ACKNOWLEDGEMENTS

Poems in this collection (some of them re-worked) are drawn from *The Sounding Circle* (Rondo, 1975), *Sinerva and Other Poems* (Headland, 1977), *The Snow Bird Sequence* (Headland, 1983), *Stoat, in Winter* (Priapus Press, 1984), *Liverpool Folio* (Duckworth, 1984) and *Studies in Stone* (Windows, 1985).

Other poems were first published in the following journals and anthologies: *Ambit, New Poetry 7* (Arts Council/P.E.N./Hutchinson), *Orbis, Osiris* (U.S.A.), *Outposts, Poetry Dimension Annual* (Ed. Dannie Abse), *Poetry Review, Poetry Wales, A Package of Poems* (Nexus Publications, 1984), *Prizewinners 1984* National Poetry Competition (The Poetry Society, 1985), *The Thomas Hardy Society Review*, 1981, *Vision On* (Ver Poets). A number of the poems have been broadcast on *BBC Radio Merseyside, BBC Radio Shropshire, Radio City,* and recorded by Gladys Mary Coles for Dial-a-Poem (051 486 2852).

The author gratefully acknowledges the support of the Welsh Arts Council who awarded her a major bursary for a period of full-time writing which enabled many of these poems to be written.

The source for 'After Edgehill, 1642' is two pamphlets printed by Thomas Jackson (London) a few months after the battle — *The Late Apparitions* and *The New Yeares Wonder* — now in the British Library, Thomason Tracts.

The following poems were major prizewinners:
'After Edgehill, 1642' in the 1986 Cardiff International Poetry Competition.
'Apprenticeship' in the 1984 National Poetry Competition (The Poetry Society/ BBC Radio 3).
'As Mad as a Hatter's Child' in the 1983 International Poetry Competition (sponsored by P.E.N., the Nuffield Foundation, Lloyds Bank for the National Schizophrenia Fellowship).
'Katherine Mansfield's Mirror' won First Prize in the Michael Johnson Memorial Poetry Competition, 1982. 'Fox' and 'Thomas Hardy at an Ambulance Society Lecture' were prizewinners in the same competition in 1976 and 1979.
'Quest' won First Prize in the Colbay International Poetry Competition, 1981.
'The Plaster Madonna' and 'Song of the Cornovii' won Lake Aske Memorial Awards, and for 'Sinerva' Gladys Mary Coles was awarded the Felicia Hemans Prize (University of Liverpool 1971-72).
'Leafburners' was read for Laurie Lee in 'A Celebration for Laurie Lee' at the 1986 Cheltenham Festival of Literature.

Cover illustration: folio 135 (Antichrist and Philosophy), the Velislav Bible (circa 1340), University Library, Prague, reproduced by courtesy of Liverpool City Libraries from Miloslav Bohatec, *Illuminated Manuscripts* (Artia, Prague, 1970).

CONTENTS

New Poems

Leafburners	10
Black Harvest	11
After Edgehill, 1642:	
1. Villagers report *The Late Apparitions*	12
2. A Ghost Speaks	12
3. A Dragoon Observes Colonel Cromwell	13
Quo Vadis?	14
Three Poems to Katherine Mansfield:	
1. Katherine Mansfield's Mirror	15
2. 'This Nettle, Danger'	16
3. Poem for Jeanne	17
The Life of a Russian Emigré	18
From the Hotel Gothart, Luzern	19
Double Take	20
Intimates	
1. The Posedown	21
2. Apprenticeship	22
3. House Party Games	23
4. As Mad as a Hatter's Child	24
Wordsworth's Umbrella	25
Quest	26
A Biographer's Visit to the Novelist's Brother	27
The Glass Island:	
1. The Legends	28
2. The Well	28
3. The Tor	29

from *The Sounding Circle* (1975)

Three Poems for Vladimir Zaaloff, Maître d'Armes:	
1. Boyhood in Georgia	32
2. Youth's Duel	34
3. Captivity, 1916	34
Bomere, Shropshire	35
Hour Glass	36
Journey, London to Cambridge	37
Midsummer and Moses	38
The Sounding Circle	39
Of Becket — from an Island in Weston Bay	40
Someone Else's Love Letter from Japan	42

Masks	43
Mandala	44
New Year's Eve	45
Sargasso	46
Death of a Frenchman	47
Consummatum Est	48

from *Sinerva and Other Poems* (1977)

Antarktikos	50
Sequence to Thomas Hardy:	
1. His Study	52
2. His Emma	53
3. At an Ambulance Society Lecture, 1882	54
In Praising Darkness	55
Parnassus	56
Song of the Cornovii	57
from Sinerva	58
Priory Ruins, Much Wenlock	60

from *The Snow Bird Sequence* (1983)

'Sing snow bird . . .'	62
'In these moon-dipped mountains . . .'	63
'One morning (after the loving) . . .'	64

from *Stoat, in Winter* (1984)

Stoat, in Winter	66
On Offa's Dyke	67
Llyn Brenig	68
Fox	69

from *Liverpool Folio* (1984)

The Coming in of Ancestors	72
A Liverpool Dock, 1982	73
The Plaster Madonna	74
Ithaca-Liverpool	75
Timepiece	76
Shop Window Models	77
On a Cobbler's Shelf	78
The Pond, West Kirby Cliffs	79
From Hilbre Island	80

from *Studies in Stone* (1985)

Studies in Stone	82
Eidyllion	83
Rock Chapel, Clwydian Hills	84
Castle Shapes, Clwydian Hills	85
Winter in Clwyd: A Sequence	86
N44, France: Holiday Route	88
Michelangelo's David	89
At Haworth	90
My Jade King	91
Gargoyles	92

New Poems

Leafburners

move quietly as smoke
to their mounds; brush
rhythmically, apply spikes
to the invoices of winter,
papery tokens of decay

others wield spades like spoons
with the ease of breakfasters
shovelling cornflakes

when the pyre is high
they strike matches avidly:
in the wind of flames
dry leaves curl, given movement
for the last time

usually at dusk, gathering
in the corners of gardens,
servants to impalpable fire
they feed the autumn bier

eyes blazing with immolation,
their office skills, creeds, degrees
fall away, severed boughs
tossed to crackle, burn
and, in burning, change

the earth the air receives

Black Harvest

All morning farmers have torn the air
gathering in a black harvest,
the grey Welsh Sunday oppressive
with sporadic gunfire, falling flesh and feathers.

We chance the metal shot, approach cornfields
where yesterday wind-light glanced and glided
beneath a moored kestrel, herons' flightpath.

Facing us, beneath a rood-screen hedge
a farmer opens his cool tabernacle,
takes bread and wine.

After Edgehill, 1642
(for Peter Holmes)

1. **Villagers Report** *The Late Apparitions*

A December Saturday, star-clear,
at Kineton. Three months since the battle,
the village collects itself — Christmas
perhaps a demarcation, a control
in the blood-letting. Yet on the ridge
of Edge Hill, the night resounds,
armies grinding one against the other
re-enacting the action, re-dying the deaths.

Shepherds hear trumpets, drums —
expect a visitation of holy kings with retinues.
Instead, the spectral soldiers strike,
icy night skies crack with cries,
steel clashing and the sput of muskets.
A knot of Kineton men watch, witness;
Samuel Marshall, the Minister, says
the Devil's apparitions seize the dead.

2. **A Ghost Speaks**

I am unplanted, my world this waste —
the heath where bone was split, undressed of flesh,
where arteries unleashed their flood, the colour
of death. What is the colour of honour? The blue
in which we dissolve into air? the white of ashes?
Can I be woven into the braids of her hair, my lady,
or exist in the quick of my son's fingernails?
I, who carried the Standard, once drove the plough,
turning up earth, the harvest of worms. Now I envy
the seeds in the furrow, their dark cradle.

My blood is this Midlands field, this hacked hedgerow
where I lie, hearing the drumbeat of the dead,
corpses strewn rotting, graveless.
I glide up and down these rows of human manure,
the faces of soldiers like fallen cameos.
Here is Sir Edmund Verney, Thomas Transome —
they look skywards, lolling near my own wistful face.
Sir Edmund is grimacing slightly as he did in life,
Thomas Transome's skull a broken eggshell.

The brittle linnet flies from me. Dry leaves relinquish
their hold on twigs. A hare sits motionless, watching,
listening to last groans forever in the wind.
I see a troop of Horse on the skyline — Parliament's.
They charge our pikemen; now they vanish
like moving cloud-shadows across the field.
I cannot follow the clouds; I am chained to my carcass
hovering, as others are, above their unburied selves.

3. A Dragoon Observes Colonel Cromwell

Like a falcon from the gauntlet, he throws off these deaths.
He tells us 'Smile out to God in Praise', for his is the sword
of the Lord. I see his horse, piebald with blood.

Quo Vadis?

It began as an ordinary country walk:
a spring evening: up to the hilltop farm —
"Lettuces For Sale". Sunday silence settled
on the fields. All day the chapels exhaled
their sleepy breath over the landscape. Three
in the steep lane: I, my children, seeking
hedgebank bluebells, their crisp promise
of summer, succulent stalks, curly caps.
Heartmagic. But questions hung in the air:

a silent one from Lynne —
she, the elder, coming through her first hell —
'*Will* all be well?'
Young Kathryn, watching a nesting blackbird,
solemnly asked, and suddenly:
'*Is* there an afterlife?'
I wanted to pluck answers from the earth
like flowers, in sure succession. Instead, uncertainty
clung, wavering like sheep's wool on the thorn.
Sounds of churchbells drifted — carried, then impeded
by the wind. Abruptly the air became thick with cries —
lambs imitating their mothers, crows flapping.

Then we saw it: where the hedge ended
and barbed wire began. A crucifixion —
three dead moles hanging, suspended by their jaws.
Shocked, we stared at the three pronged bodies,
their paws — little pink-gloved hands — outstretched.
Varying in size, they might have been a family,
executed as a warning to all who tunnel
for survival, or answers.

THREE POEMS TO KATHERINE MANSFIELD

Katherine Mansfield's Mirror (Châlet des Sapins)

A chalet of the old type, cuckoo-clock roof,
ornate, the balcony creaking;
and the view she saw each day
across to the Weisshorn above Sierre —
these I saw too, as with her eyes.
The perpetual snows, the vines in neat plots:
it's hardly changed at all since she was there,
since her bid to cure her lungs in Alpine air.
'Oui, c'est le même,' the concierge nods,
key-laden, at the door, *'aussi les sapins'*.
Evergreens, omnipresent, guard the chalet —
'the last romantic thing left in Montana'
wryly the concierge smiles, takes me up
to Katherine's room, her balcony, her mirror.
The mirror in its wooden frame
on a wall between two windows:
I move forward eagerly, look — and look away,
and cannot stand in front, not wanting to imprint
my own reflection on this glass. It should be kept
unlooked in, any vestige of her glance preserved
like the high snows, unvisited and pure.
And then a deeper reason shows its face:
I am afraid: in this mirror at her disease
she stared, seeking the trace of a Colonial girl
in the troughs of her dark eyes. My own lungs
weak, prey to the wheeze of allergy, I fear
her stark reality in that mirror: in there
I might fall and sink, be swallowed
in her consuming truth.

'This Nettle, Danger'*

at Fontainebleau early light
filters the forest screen
cigarette smoke drifts
through crumbling shutters

December winds stir the lake
brushing the taut timpano
moving lethargic pines
to cough and rasp, dying
their long death, grey
tattered lines of ragged
knickers

in the darkest foliage
scarlet berries spilled
like blood beads —
here the nettles, black mass
thick as Gurdjieff's beard,
will multiply in spring
holding their secret
within the latent sting

on sandy paths residual snow —
lake-edge blanched like the foamy
beach at Menton, sheets of washerwomen
white banners in cobbled yards:
a world ago that Mediterranean sun,
the orange groves, those purring afternoons,
aromatic evenings, art the anodyne

now winter boughs encircle the lake
where Lamartine once wept for his lady
with the burnt-out lungs

---

*from the Shakespearean inscription on Katherine Mansfield's gravestone at Fontainebleau, where she died 9th January, 1923.

Poem for Jeanne
(born 20 May, 1892, sister of Katherine Mansfield)

At Wellington the southerly busters blow
from the straits, deepening the harbour's bite,
flattening grasses on the Tinakori hills —
these, and the bent manuka trees
are as you remember, like the elements
unchanged. And other essentials:
the toi-toi, waving its head-dress
like a Maori chieftain; Alpine heights
and boiling springs; the surrounding surf,
its scarves of mist and spray;
yellow-fruited Karakas; and the ever-elusive
Kiwi. You tell me, as if to convince yourself,
that you've made your last return —
all is held in the mind. Memory's cargo
wrapped and bound. Yet at times you strive
to recall a family's laughter, Father's wit,
your sisters' competitive company, the smile
of a soldier brother, dead in France.

From your window now, you watch
a great wind agitating the beech trees
which stand at a polite distance
across these Gloucestershire lawns.
Katherine's writings are on your bookshelf —
and in your mind; the family gathers round
in photographs, with a few remnants
of your elegant home. Always positive,
you smile, describe the Home as a large liner
each voyager in a single cabin:
at night, all windows lit,
your ship slides into Wellington harbour.

The Life of a Russian Emigré
(Vladimir Zaaloff, Maître d'Armes)

He thought he understood the Revolution
even though — tutor to the Tsar's court
in three weapons — no one believed him
or listened, least of all his Bolshevik captors.
All too clear those last days in Petrograd —
the confusion and the shouting, gunshots,
crowds storming the Schlüsselburg.
He'd known in early September — the air rife
with rumour, the radical end of summer
approaching, scuffed leaves in Uritzky Square —
the Revolution was irreversible,
'Peace, Land, Bread' the cry everywhere.

No aristocrat himself (from a village in Georgia
where his father withered on towards a hundred, watched
by his mother, careful of bad meat, icons, wolves)
he thought he understood the Revolution,
witnessed the assassination of Rasputin.
But carrying no party card he was arrested,
swords an anachronism before the Red Guards' guns.

That escape through the high, slit window, a fall
of twenty feet, he'd only just managed, running
in darkness along the Moyka. Hidden a month
by cousin Nadya — *'Skoro! Skoro!'* she whispered
as he left, sliding at night across the flatlands.
Finland at dawn. A boat to Aberdeen. The drift south
to exile in London. A language to be learnt
while the old language of steel gave him a living.

Familiar music, this clash of foils, épees,
the crueller sound of sabres. Physical chess
in Balham; tuned muscles; the generations.
Not to anyone did he speak of the Revolution —
not even to Lydia, his wife for a while, singer
in 'The Balalaika' when he danced, black eyes blazing.
A robot bomb in the next War claimed
the framed photographs — Nadya, her son Grigori,
his father at a hundred. Layers of winters since,
yet old wounds beneath the snow, ready to flame
like Siberian flowers.

From the Hotel Gothart, Luzern

1. This pale Midlands woman in our party
   sits at the table on her second night abroad
   her first time away from England and her children.
   She frowns at the smoked meat, the capucinno,
   says a cold sore on her lip is troubling her.
   Outside the air is tranquil: all summer
   Switzerland has been hugged in cloud.
   Frau Bosch, as she brings the drinks, tells us
   of fog, extraordinary for the season,
   explaining guiltily, apologising as though
   she had made it herself from a mist-machine.
   Her husband sits smoking by the open door
   his cheeks russet and glazed
   like the apple shot by William Tell.

2. Our room overlooking the lake
   is an enormous cupboard; its wood glistens
   richly, and creaks whenever a train thrusts
   along the lakeside — tracks, metallic energy
   out of place in this immensity of water.
   The cracked bell tolls at eight: we embark
   in the chartered launch. Nori and Mitzi
   cradle cameras, constantly clicking
   on leave from *Sony,* Basingstoke and Tokyo.
   Stout lonely Ted has seen it all before —
   acts as surrogate guide, spoils our surprises,
   tells us not to expect the snow-cusped
   Bristenstock, a recluse in cloud.

3. We hear the tale of Tell, approach the shrine:
   so many suppositions in this reality of rock.
   At the Devil's Cathedral we can make suggestions
   of our own, see in the cliff face any face —
   grotesque, erotic, animal, android —
   these shapes will answer back to any call
   in any language, throw echoes of exiled desires,
   our unspeakable stored responses.
   We return for coffee. Re-load our cameras.

Double Take

Last summer I held a sweating baby in an Italian bus
   travelling from Sorrento to Sant' Agnello on the hill.
He'd writhed in his mother's arms, she'd smiled at us —
   a sad, apologetic smile — as women will

who think their child is spoiling someone's pleasure.
   Her small daughter cried and pulled her arms,
wanting to claim her, discard the baby brother:
   I took him as he shrieked his fierce alarms.

There was the Roman nose, bald brown head,
   white robe wrapping the distended belly
of this mini Julius Caesar whom I held
   struggling for his Empire — his mother's body.

His usurping sister ruled the breasts and knees,
   gripping tight as we swung up from the Marina Grande.
He fixed his gaze on me and clutched my necklace;
   I asked his name — she answered, 'Salvatore'.

Last summer I sketched an old man at an Italian beach:
   he sat toad-like under the bamboo of a pier café
day after day in the same seat, looking down at each
   young swimmer bronzing the turquoise Tirreno Mare.

With my conté I caught the Roman nose, bald brown head,
   white robe wrapping the distended belly
of this aged Julius Caesar whom I held
   in my gaze, as he surveyed his Empire — a balcony

high on the harbour flats, and a woman in black
   to whom he slowly waved from time to time
and who, from time to time, waved back
   bridging the distance in a mirrored mime.

Aware of a posture shift, he smiled apologetically
   between surreptitious sips of his *acqua minerale,*
while inquisitive locals gathering round excitedly
   examined the likeness and shouted 'Salvatore!'

INTIMATES

The Posedown

Without my glasses I can't see the audience or judges
but I hear the reaction as I flex my oiled bunches
solid as Spanish onions, shiny as conkers.
In the glass Superdrome I'm hoping to make the posedown,
to figure prominently in the Middleweight division.
My striations are sure to please. Today my definition's
clearer than ever before, torso muscles honed —
in sharp detail. The last six weeks self-sculpting,
ripping off (see my ribbed veins), regime of iron,
liver liquid, anabolic packs, has certainly paid off
moulding my Michelangelo manshape.

I'm pumping up now. Five strung-out minutes until
they call the top six. I just know I'll be selected,
onstage again, performing (as Schwarzenneger says) my art.
This thigh pose should stop the show, and here's
my ultimate creative position. It's a pity though
that Sonia dislikes my skin — 'like overdone sirloin'.
Nasty, that. No excuse, even if she is vegetarian
and breeds prize Siamese. Jealous as well, maybe,
knowing how Julie admires my deltoid routine, oils
my double biceps. But Sonia gives me no back-up
not even nutritional, neglecting my collagen, my adrenal
hormones. Julie though, after workout, is always there
feeding me dessert spoons of raw amino elixir.
This won't do. I must concentrate on myself, project
my mental prime. I've peaked on time. Confidence
is all I need to win. If I do, Julie's promised me
that blue dumbell kit. The names are being called . . .
'Jane Phipps'. Yippee!

Apprenticeship

While I sat on the hay bales adjusting
my cap tighter, Fitzgerald — he's our Trainer —
spoke snappily, his elastic voice twanging
(a Newry larynx, gift of generations
together with equine know-how).
His fur hat was a split black-pudding —
Russian, the kind donned by academics —
his old sheepskin coat was sausage rings.
We shivered as we mounted in the dawn,
my hands cold on the warm flanks of the gelding,
later warm on its cold sweat froth.
After we finished the exercise, as always
Fitzgerald made his points, poking the air,
chipolata fingers around a cigar. 'Be sure now
to towel up. See you back here at the usual time.'

In the ice-box of the dormitory, its one electric bar
giving a thin heat, I changed my woollen vest,
ignoring the ridicule by the lads. At breakfast
I took second helpings. 'You won't make the weight!'
Maybe, but I don't care. I think of Michael Reid —
Grandfather's brother, orphaned at nine,
apprenticed as a jockey at eleven. He needed to be small
to live. Kept himself light, went lighter.
Returning from Chantilly, he leapt onto a train,
choked in his own red froth. I remember Michael
when I see Fitzgerald's mouth, every day,
spilling red ash at the end of his corona.

House Party Games

August afternoon. Sky battleship grey.
Devon valley drizzle seeping all day.
We hung over the Aga, warmed our hands,
drank mulled wine, talked of Agamemnon.
'Backgammon?' my host suggested. I agreed.
In the parlour we moved our men tactically
on the war-board. Poking logs, raking ash
he told me his wife was leaving him.
I heard her in the kitchen shuffling cups,
reluctantly shredding meat for guests.
Then, 'Look, the rain has stopped!' —
the cry spilled from children, untamed
as farm kittens, hurtling into the yard.
'Badminton?' my host suggested. I agreed.

Setting the net outside
we tentatively played first shots.
'She's going soon', he said. Overhead
the shuttle moved. I missed, then lightly
served to counterfeit some joy. Higher
higher again, we set the shuttle soaring
on nylon wings. Soon, phut into the net
like a captured bird. Startled in nearby trees
white pigeons whirled. Panic rise from boughs,
dazzle of sun in rain-clear air: which was shuttle
which was bird? Over and back, my host hit harder,
smashed a feathered being at my feet.

We heard her Mini throating down the lane,
the air empty of birds
the manger empty of beasts
the yard empty of children
a toy helicopter sticking in the mud
two dying lettuces without hearts
splayed like fallen flags across the soil.

As Mad As A Hatter's Child

Our first two were dead born
like strangled lambs, their movements
ceasing weeks before, small deaths
hidden and silent, causing no stir.
Since then, years of hat-making, orders
from all Salisbury and beyond. The triumph
of the Lord Mayor's new topper —
I glossed it, shiny as a mare's flank;
my wife used it as a mirror.
Councillors and corn-merchants gave me custom
vying with each other for bowlers
worn at the Queen's Jubilee celebrations
above bellies as round as barrels.

Our little Emily came four summers back.
A lily child, white and gold,
perfect in all her limbs and face.
How we rejoiced that August, into harvest,
taking the babe on woodland walks.
We gathered by the great West Door
for her christening in the Cathedral,
cloisters thronged with our men-folk,
women best-bonnetted and gowned.
The spire shone white against the blue,
distant fields glowed with ungathered wheat.

Yesterday we gathered again, hatted and cloaked,
for her March burial among daffodils.
Those yellow heads bobbing in a cold wind
mocked me: so had my Emily danced, deranged
at the whim of her brain's wild jigging.
Crazed she grew, crawling and threshing.
O, our Lord God, was this Thy will?
Was it a sin to take her to the wizard
hoping the wise one could cast out
her demon, reverse the spell of madness?
Nothing succeeded — neither the wizard's word-chain,
nor charms, nor the Bishop's prayers.
Fever took her at last, and her lily spirit
now rests, I like to think,
pale and golden
on some sheltered lake.

*Derangement now known to be caused by chemicals used in the polishing process.

Wordsworth's Umbrella

A parasol for the rain, large enough to accommodate
wet friends — De Quincey, Southey — or the household
women. Often it sheltered Dorothy as they walked
in lanes and fields of seeping hues:
the hilltops came and went under cloud,
water feeding the lakes, the lakes the land.

Lichen-coloured now, it's out of the damp,
a museum companion to the cloak and hat;
nearby, another record of lakeland days —
Coleridge's 'Ode to the Rain', in notebook hand.

I emerge again into insistent drizzle,
anoraked, watching the walkers in kagoules,
harsh colours against the subtle Grasmere greens.
That verdigree umbrella, giant fungus, blended
far better with this scene, aesthetic adjunct
to arthritic trees. I sneeze, reminded of Dorothy's
'Wm. slept ill. A soaking all-day rain';
of William's *'The rain came heavily and fell in floods';*
and how she dried his hair before the peat fire
steadily glowing, the heart of their house place.
So powerful the link, the lakes seem theirs.

It recalls Ambleside, a honeymoon:
our future seemed as vast as Windermere
though misty at the edge;
in happy student poverty we walked
great lengths, wet fells, close under his umbrella —
our sole house place in those first days.
Since then, showers, monsoons:
the lakes absorb them and remain unchanged.
Returning now, I celebrate to find
an ancient umbrella and the same fine rain.

Quest

Life, its thrust and pith,
surrounds in this town's heart,
pounds, pitches every purchased moment
forward to the next.

Finding the sanctuary
I enter its healing air,
balm of old books, quiet
of antiques, mirrored residue of life
lived yet not quite gone,
pot-pourri of other people's past.

Deciduous dust beckons.
I touch the time-spots:
books like tomb-stones
of dead authors —
some the nameless names,
words preserved yet unpreserving;
but here and there a Wordsworth, Dickens,
Shakespeare, even a Lamb's *Tales of*
and *Seven Pillars of Wisdom*.

Aspiring to be among their company
in a volume crumbling to dust,
I am seeking a book
to help me to write
a book I've been writing
about a woman who wrote books
(a long time dead).

I look in the box-loads
brought here after the hearse
has left, after the auctioneer's voice,
after the relatives' choice.

I am searching for a book
to help me to write a book
that might be read
and perhaps not forgotten
when I am dead.

A Biographer's Visit to the Novelist's Brother

He cares for bees, harvests honey
scraping a living and beeswax
from the comb; cultivates new swarms
in this colony of small citadels.
Forty hives and a hut
his world, as hers was the hills,
the valleys, the meres of a landscape
outer and inner. His sister
dead half a lifetime ago, yet alive
in her words. I ask him questions
gently at first, on matters of pain —
my probes persistent bees hovering
over the prized pollen, the nectar.
But family secrets remain locked
like the queen in the hive.

He invites me in to tea. Sweetness
of his own produce and a honey light
oozing through the opaque window.
His age-freckled hand pours cream.
I try again: 'Do you remember . . .'
and 'What was her reaction when . . .'
Eyes, the faint blue of Roman glass,
concentrate, evade. Instead, he recounts
a family story, embellished in the telling,
relishing the humour, my response.

Facts from fifty years are stored
as the contents of bee cells —
sealed, inaccessible.
I correct some dates for him,
reveal the researched background.
'Well!' he laughs, 'you've been scouring
the honeycomb. You know more about my family
than I do myself.'

The Glass Island
(*Yns-Witrin* or Glastonbury)

1. The Legends

A green lagoon; marshes, reed-mazed,
and a long boat gliding like the swans,
the quiet swans drawing their invisible chariot
towards the otherworld, the glass island.

And the long boat arriving nudges the grassy banks
where the only sound is the whispered sound
of voyagers from a time before, their circular call
to those, water-crossing, who come ashore.

Centuries of comings, season by season —
the grail-seekers, the pilgrims
leaving no trace on light and air.

The white perpetuation of belief:
a midwinter thorn blossoming
each ice-time in the melt-meadows;
a windfall of bones in a buried oak
'here lies Arthur and golden Guinevere'.

Words and wood and water —
water a reservoir of beginnings
speaking of pre-beginnings.

2. The Well

A liquid torc around the neck
of a pilgrim, reflected, drinking
from the chalice of earth.

3. The Tor

Rising above other domes of grass,
above Wearyall and Windmill,
the island of glass under an unreal geography
of clouds, shape-shifting, pulled apart.
Cloud-drift, constantly dispersing,
reassembling, like the seekers who come
season by turning season: they wind
a spiral way up vestigial paths
and fade one by one
imperceptibly as the wild geese
flying high at twilight.

Heat, marsh-light and the glass island
glistening behind the sun's incense.
What shines is neither grail nor chalice
but sharp-edged shards, a glazed bead
a fragment of window, water in a glass.

from

The Sounding Circle

THREE POEMS FOR VLADIMIR ZAALOFF, MAÎTRE D'ARMES
(born 1894)

Boyhood in Georgia

'He'll be a fine boy with good lungs . . .' — Gogol

Village older than rococo,
curled in heat. Summer
stilled as a water-wheel
no water turning.
Pigs asleep in the sun
painted in light
like a craftsman's carvings
of plump angels sold
at a trestle table. Sameness

real as the unreality
of ikons, spiritually pregnant.
A scholar pushes his cart
to market, knowledge word-wrapped.
It is too hot
for clothed knowledge.

Lisp of wind, a prophetic bell
intimate winter:

first snowflakes drift
on time. We accept
a frozen eternity, learn
to dance in barns, watch
storm twisting limbs
of the bare-boned forest.
Icicles — our swords — exhilarate,
cool hot mouths, cut
the roots of childhood.

We wrestle, jump, send laughter
tolling in the rafters:
the house an empty church
two finger-candles burning
at the rime-white window.

Nikolai lies, grinning, on a catafalque:
we four, his Cossack guards, whisper
of Tzaricide, blood
on hard-packed snow, assassination
of Alexander and an errand boy,
afternoon death in a parcel —
white to red, smoke shroud of slaughter,
men severed from horses, legs from men.

We use our legs, leap, vault
to prove they still belong to our bodies.
'The Emperor has bidden you live long!'
We are rebels without a rebellion.

Shadow changes on the steppes:
already shoots push
higher than the soil.

Youth's Duel

Weapons chosen, we salute each other,
observe politeness at the point of death
intent on graceful execution: he tests
his sword-edge; I, the tension of my blade.

On guard. The age-old engagement. One to one.
Unaware of universals, only the particulars
of tensile steel. Feint of attack and counter;
doublé and riposte; bluff and counter-bluff.
React. React. Exact.

No time to think how Pushkin died.
Children of the she-bear
(neither Russian poets nor Russian Christs) —
earth the womb or earth the tomb?

Captivity, 1916

Thoughts break loose
from some locked cell
streaming towards
one shining synthesis:

like Tolstoy's white-breasted swallows
flying with whirling grain
out of the dusky barn at Polyana
bright-flapping in the light
above the dark and toiling peasants.

Thoughts might die
in some locked cell.

Bomere, Shropshire
(to Mary Webb)

Rings of aged bark
conceal this dark mere,
recipient of life;

muted, the bells in its core
unsounded, drowned
with the village, lost
in the swallowing well
unfathomable as the black hole
of a collapsed star.

Linked trees hold
the spell:
tall lichened alchemists
distilling a special silence,
permitting particular sounds.

Listen! You might hear
the breath of time

whispered in the sipping
of the mere, liquid lips
incessant
to the dipped boughs;
echoed in rooks' raw cries,
contractions of pathos
answered by the bittern
or a solitary heron
objectively fashioning
its reflection;

and ever the hint
of leaf music,
soundless sigh of roots,
mashy moist of earth
becoming mud,
dispersing.

Hour Glass

Consider the shape of an hour glass —
the constant flow
from rounded upper to rounded lower,
the balance held
in that narrow channel span
where falls each individual grain
from the full and crystal bowl
inevitably to the waiting lower sphere,
and every falling grain
the total sand receives.
Shape of glass to corresponding glass,
lower to upper and again the same.

Consider the sands of an hour glass,
creating their own tide
which knows no late or soon,
which cannot wash away
or cover the shells,
obeys no moon.

Journey — London to Cambridge

What reality exists in this, to sit
in a mechanised glow-worm, creeping
out from the concrete forest
under a dark December dawn?
Strange, yet less than strange
to see these passing homes,
their safety of nestled stone
and security of lights in breakfast windows,
sped and gone,
sped and gone like meteorites,
an unreal backcloth spun off the reel of time
with no re-wind.

What vitality exists in this, to see
the houses like frosted bun-loaves
line the shelves of winter fields
where charcoaled whiteness gleams?
And there they huddle in the dawn
as neighbour trees in copses
rooted, drained by a night network.
Sad, yet less than sad
to know we flit
small burdened sparrows
drawn by light into a great hall
in and out
in and out of windows with no glass.

Midsummer and Moses

Fires of unremembered summers
blaze heart high
in my burning bush
as I, beneath the shadow roses,
think of midsummer and Moses.

Flames of unremembered leaves
on this side and on that
mutely pattern time upon the grass:
so do my thoughts elide
then dart and skim
like antique Egyptian flies
along the green rim
of the Nile, among those guardian rushes
sheltering the secret water cradle.

Flickering beginnings
as Moses, saved for destiny,
later, on hot Mount Horeb heard
the consuming voice in the burning bush.
I, too, listen, since my bush is flaming,
but this is no sacred mountain,
no exodus awaits me,
I must create my own book of numbers,
need no tablets of stone.

Myth in undertides stirs deeply yet,
rises to new forms, renewing
with the leaves, the grass, the roses —
so Freud, in Rome, seeing the stone Moses
envisaged a primal father
Michelangelo carved yet never conceived;

and I, turning my inward hearing
to the burning bush, listen
in my patch of midsummer.

The Sounding Circle

"an infinite sphere, centre everywhere,
circumference nowhere."
— Hermes Trismegistus

Listening inwardly
I hear a finer singing
like the song of unseen seals
or the distant Sirens of Hellas
caught in the lulls
and pauses of earth's rumour,
in the wider murmur of the sea.

It is rhythmic
as punctual tides
are rhythmic;

it sings of a truth
that was and is
as primordial as death;

not new and never old
it sounds

in the sounding circle.

Of Becket — from an Island in Weston Bay

Children, coming to Flat Holme, ask
when did these die
and why were they important?
If parents know the answers
they reply that here under ancient mounds
on an offshore island lie
those doomed knights, their skeletal bones,
skulls, dust;

others, who have consulted and trust
detailed historical texts, hold
past intricacies as present fact: cultured
they can relive the act
of murder seen as mythic drama (imbued
with symbols, it nourishes, entertains) —
sufficient to inspire an Eliot or Anouilh,
invested with significances, reverberations,
embedded meanings and interpretations;
sensational as Hamlet's death,
the last sad cry of Antigone,
Gatsby's end or that of mad Macbeth.

Yet children wonder still
confronted by a strange calligraphy,
why the knights were doomed
who entombed them here
under the sea-light and the salty soil.
Thinking to educate the young,
those with stored knowledge tell
how Thomas fell, how Henry played
the Judas game, and these same knights
in the grey light of a cathedral came
unsheathing death into sinew, into breath,
made holy bones of Becket
Archbishop, martyr, man.

And if in future time
the children span a decade or three
there still will be these mounds
on a mound in the sea
telling of blood lust;
and of Becket's medieval dust, nothing,
shrine pulled apart (there was no heart)
bones cannon-blown to Tudor winds;
while at Fontevrault lies an eroded image
of an image of a king
kissed by a lasting kiss
of peace.

Someone Else's Love Letter from Japan

Fragrance —
I open a drawer
in a hotel bedroom —
and find, like a discarded petal,
someone else's love-
letter from Japan.

Tomoku from Tokyo
to Peter in London
out of touch.

Akikawa (she says)
is the river of autumn:
she has entered it
is enclosed in a temple
of faceless people
come to the stillness —

nature has been sacrificed here
('O how I wish for walks on Hampstead Heath').

The heart of the temple
is a cold abstract:

one part of it is new
('O how I detest the new')
new building, new city
new love, new pain;

the air is polluted
except in the temple;

leaves fall on Hampstead Heath
as love falls
into the waste
paper basket —
someone else's letter
from Japan.

Masks

I am wearing
a ritual mask
at a funeral feast
that is becoming
familiar

I am skilled
at mumming and miming
yet my mask
crackles like a paper clown's
and will melt
if tear-sodden
at the appropriate hour

there is ice
in my crystal glass
it has been chipped
from your iceberg

it freezes the wine

Mandala

Clothed in winter lichens
trees, attentive for Spring,
are luminous rings
still as points in spirals.

Blackbirds seem protrusive
dense, ponderous-winged
bungling among branches
grown ethereal
viridian-veiled
sheer suspense
in slightest twig.

No nest, no leaf intrudes:
while breathing seems
a discord, lichens move

yet imperceptibly.

New Year's Eve

Shake of stars and frost shine
clear darkness
dilating in the eye of night
as the year shrinks
to the hooting of a ship's owl,
fog call of the far-off,
bark of death's dog,
enigmatic chiming of the mystery clock
and auld lang syne
wrung from the tilting throat
of present life
fated to spin
in a mote of time.

And the cold moon staring
at old earth travelling, turning
travelling on:

the eye in the maelstrom
eternally drowning.

A child cries Mother!
Father!

Sargasso

Give me a dark night in Spring,
tall wet grasses, meadows of mud
and I will leave my pond —
so shallow, stale and still —
and slide, silvery, to the sea.
Remotely memoried, remotely within
is my circular dream:
O, I must follow the dream —
coil, release, return
yes, follow the dream.
And the singing streams call
with the stones that gleam like bones:
these, and the lisping leaves repeat
'Follow the dream'.

Give me the swelling tides
to ride me to the deeps.
I came like a water leaf,
transparent, thin
from the far shelving seas of spawn.
Let me return
to the liquid abyss,
to the radiant death,
to Sargasso.

Death of a Frenchman

Paris. Reflections riot in the Seine.
At Notre Dame the cardinal archbishop
intones, in accents of Auvergne,
an ancient requiem. Gathered in gloom

like dark bewildered birds, men of power
and public honour contemplate this passing
of a man of power and public honour.
Total eclipse: the hour of confusion:
dawn and dusk chorus heard together.
A Bach chorale and De Profundis.
Only the priests possess illusory splendour —

hooded albs, gilded stoles and gold of hollow
chalices staining their faces, they wield
in measured solemnity, to and fro, the silver
sacramental thuribles. Incense pervades
the chancel, tenuous as hope.

A river wind rises, strengthens,
stirs all the trees of Paris
to plainsong.

Consummatum Est

An empty circle of sand
set in a tiered ring:

death's jewel gleams
in the mind,
darkly red as the eyes
of a fated bull.

In the sleep-sated town
hot, crowded, expectant,
thousands await
this blood feast,
prepare to celebrate
a mystery, offer
the sacrificial beast;

ceremonially clothed
high priest of the ritual,
sanctified by courage
the matador looks long
at his mirror image:

beauty, grace of form,
lyrical energy of movement
at one with the dark menace
circling, passing, circling
to still the flesh

and letting out blood
let life in.

from

Sinerva and Other Poems

Antarktikos

(Greek: the land on the side of the world opposite 'the bear')

Lured to the polar base of earth
drawn to this vast white womb,
man, here, can be no lord
of territory where ice shelves
move inevitably to sea;
where countless cold peaks and shapes
rise jaggedly in frost-smoke.

Anywhere is north from here.
Time, like direction, has strange
meanings — now total dark,
now total light, there's continuous day
or constant night — locked in ice,
locked outside time, clocks
are neither wrong nor right.

Relics remind of previous life:
petrified trees, stone images of forest,
flowers, suggest primordial warmth;
burnt-out fires of ghost towns —
dwellings with forgotten chattels
like a pharoah's tomb — abandoned
to the desert of drifting snow;
and man-made caves given back
to the conquering, encircling ice.

Always ahead, barking of dogs,
voices of men welcome in any tongue:
the invader knows he's prisoner
of the polar plateau draped deep
in ancient ice and centuries' snow —
lost in this alien hemisphere
he's soon a frozen effigy.

To be able to survive, existence
must be artificial. An artificial peace?
Twelve nations and no boundaries.
Illimitable ice but no Cold War.
Low temperatures, warm interchange,
century-old germs in deep freeze.

Purely scientific. The specialist, though intent,
breathes carefully for fear of frozen lungs,
impelled to examine every living thing,
fix algae, focus lichen, dissect fish
(garnering facts for files). Aware
that fingers might numb, scientists
paint numbers on penguins, swab
throats of soft-eyed seals, stain
this sea-bird red, that a livid green.
Yet rocks, fossils, bone hold the unknown
like white tracts of an uncharted map.

Reminders of civilised continents? . . . Perhaps
those jostling penguins in formal black and white
who toss a colleague to the killer seal
and thereby test the safety of deep waters;
or the threshing packs of vicious mammals
that stalk in stinging seas, attack, destroy;
and the blue whale shedding giant tears.

In a landscape not his own, man tracks
the ice desert

and out of the white void
new winds come
to stir old snows.

Sequence to Thomas Hardy

1. **His Study** (Dorset County Museum)

The desk, implacable altar. Glass inkpots
without ink. Cheap pens, redundant rusty spears.
Blotter like the map of Europe: calligraphy of *Tess,
Jude,* countless ironic poems might spring
to the mirror's view. On a chair doctoral gown
and bonnet (honorary props), the needed walking stick.
Behind glass in a rural museum, his conjured ghost
sits, brooding like a walnut owl at dusk;
again in a universe of words, surveying
eight decades of life, time's outrollings
in a space cavern, whirl of planet around planet,
of flies around a cow's tail, of lover into lover.
Searchlighting an inner world, he adapts, adjusts
everything — even Stonehenge — in service
of created fate; like Napoleon

small, wry, inscrutable
manipulating destinies.
Poet poised between two voids,
by sleight of mind, hand of wife
writing his own non-autobiography —
in wrinkled fame burdened by his name,
outmanoeuvring all who would claim his Life,
strip him naked, fillet, dissect, consume
every red corpuscle of his existence,
a reality self-hewn, craftsman-carved
like the music of stone. Organ sound
of a marble grave. Thomas Hardy, O.M.

Old mandarin at verbal chess, he cheats,
pruning the factual fiction, plot of his life,
last novel with a thousand twist endings,
the final counterfeit to confine, clip
each academic sheep-shearer.

And now the glass darkens,
light loses light,
God may yet arrive.

2. His Emma

November twenty seventh, nineteen twelve.
No further turning of the days
this date fixed as on her tombstone.
Emma — she who had no use for goodbyes —
his everywhere woman, espoused ghost.
He hears her voiceless calling
down the thin winds at Lyonesse,
forever his phantom lady riding
her pale horse at the sea's margin
wind flailing her spectral hair
sea-birds bearing the wild salt spirit
perhaps to cessation.

Or sometimes he sees her swaying, silent
on tide-wet rocks, forty years of tears falling;
and again, interminably at her piano
fingering lost tunes. Estranged in life
she was already the ghost beyond grasp
to him who understood less but knew more
of all the tenses of their marriage
than this now forever pluperfect
of the never perfect.
November twenty seventh, nineteen twelve.

3. At an Ambulance Society Lecture, 1882

the audience, sitting, faces the speaker
a skeleton hangs inside the window
outside children are dancing
feet skiffing rhythmically across stones
map of bones over glass

slight figures twine to music
the skeleton dangling steals daylight
provides first and last aid for the living
and Hardy sitting — he who noticed such things —
saw the ring of bones, hollow unsexed cave
saw the ring of small dancers erotic, pulsing
like far stars in primal innocence
heard the splintered silent laughter from the skull

and the skeleton grinned
at the audience gaping
at the children dancing
at the band playing
at the fields tilting
at the world turning
at Hardy sitting
contemplating his cosmos
empty of a newly dead God
cursed for never being born

and Hardy heard the skeleton's mindless singing
watched it dance in his brain

In Praising Darkness

all metaphors
are white
in praising darkness

above forests of dust
the moon
is a pale scythe

you brought me
the trembling notes of birds
held in a clear glass

I asked you
did you hear the aspens
shake their ghostly underleaves

I am the leaf
quaking
in a dust forest

hold back the winds

Parnassus

Parnassus:
the mountain slides beneath its rain clouds,
slips from the shelf of time
as those twin peaks of oracle and muse
fold in and fuse:
the nimbus releases subtle rains of life
to an amphitheatre of waiting grasses.

The grasses:
on strands of being they bend
fronded, wistful
before the purging winds
which perform a sure abscission.
Then strays a seed
to reach some alien and sombre shore:
that once unwilling ground
knows frondescence, inner, pure.
As mists retreat into the day,
so the calyx curls away
and the corolla, whole, is found.

Song of the Cornovii*

(for Colin Haycraft)

Toadflax blazes in the rock —
a hill fort taken by grass siege

thistles rasp, bristling banners
triumph of green armour
where the last Cornovii defended:
Viricon, Vortigern gone
like the meltwaters.

Below, agencies of thrust and flow
possess the plain, more indigenous
than those tribal species, beating out
their shields of bronze, burnishing
black bowls, digging their holes
of death, lighting hill-top fires
on a not quite extinct
volcano.

More indigenous this green army
than the Latin men, dark, supple-minded,
shivering in their new white city
under snow upon snow
trying to create internal warmth
remembering, in the mosaics of a life,
hot tiles of Roman summers

while the astral ice body
of the peak
conquers glacial ground.

Underwood sounds. Echoes of violence,
cracks, explosions, fire-bursts
fracturing clouds, frictioning water
quickening wick of war:

nothing can repair
the rift in this song,
broken tree-ribs, the shattered stone

yet nothing has been subtracted.

*The Cornovii, an early British tribe living around the Wrekin, Shropshire.

from *Sinerva*

(a Finnish Myth)

White in the darkness
the frozen forests stretch
icicle-long to the moon.
Trees creak and fall
beneath the weight of snow
like stiffened Goliaths.
Lakes and land unite
under the blank coverlet
of Finnish winter.
Then reindeers shiver,
herding in the glades
of forgotten green,
the trellis of their horns
etched like thickets
sharp against the snow.
And man is quiet,
sombre, lapped in furs,
patient in the long darkness
for rebirth is near.

The peace of snow retreats;
ice diamonds crack
in the midnight sun
and spring comes — sudden,
radiant as love,
to thaw deep frozen energies.
Raunu, keen-eyed,
hermetic in his hut,
was eager for life anew.
The winter long he'd waited,
watching the inner man
old in his ageing youth.
He speared the secret fish —
swift, plunged in the quiet lake,
triangular coldness among the pines.
His thoughts were of Sinerva,
calm as the snow, crystalline,
the eternal bud unopened —

Sinerva in the young light
threading her morning tresses,
pale stream of loveliness.
Yet her remoteness clung
like fungus to his being;
tendrils of lost tenderness
choked his spirit,
strangling the harp of joy.
He walked with tireless steps
in the lake-gemmed forest,
hunting the lynx in the undergrowth
like his soul.
Purling green grew gold
in the mirror of his childhood
as Raunu, treading the moss
and the berries, beryl-brown,
listened to the leaves.
He must leave the forest,
and seek Sinerva in her village
masked by birch
crouched near the Sima lake
where swallows sleep.

*The opening section of the long poem which is published in full in *Sinerva and Other Poems*

Priory Ruins, Much Wenlock

pale roses cloistered
where white robed doves
inhabit high corridors

petal fragments fallen
in the transept
like lost psalms

my soul responds, dilates
seeing you there
in the green nave
holding a white rose
pure as Shropshire air

from

The Snow Bird Sequence

"The snow-semblanced moon-matcher"
— Dafydd ap Gwilym

'Only connect . . .' — E. M. Forster

Sing snow bird
of love
branched in the night
of a broken tree

sing silently
to me

morning's song
song of tides
softly sibilant
spiral of sea

sing snow bird
of love
sprinkle with light
this foliage of gloom
chime crystal white
your unheard tune

'Love is . . . the desire the pursuit of the whole' — Aristophanes

    In these moon-dipped mountains
    engulfed in a dense black bowl
    I want to press
    vast love prints
    on the sky
    so that you —
    enclosed in separate distance —
    can read the night
    and know
    my silent meaning.

    But the sky seems impaled
    on stars, time-speared, remote.

    I send messages
    with dun-winged birds,
    find expression
    in trees' dark gestures
    and in their secret hearts.

"without contraries is no progression" — William Blake

One morning (after the loving)
we dress, run to the bay
hearing the roar, exultant, continuous
of mingled waves wind spray —
and see the wooden groynes
along the shore. Endlessly
the groynes stretching through mist
long dark fingers grasping
the sand — protective, possessive.

Again we come, at dusk
after the sea's retreat
when the groynes seem
like black ribs of the beach —
vast grey lung silently
imperceptibly breathing.

At the shoreline, we recall
Victorian paintings of the bay:
sands toned purple-gray
sky-billowed, empty of people
only a solitary woman edging the sea
in black bonnet and wind-tossed cloak
watching ambivalently forever
a fishing boat at tilt forever;
and in other painted seas
the groynes like drowning galleons
with ruined masts and spar
yet holding still their treasure
beneath the waves.

I ask you (who can read my body
like the tides) how to secure
love, keep it from erosion
as these groynes the sand?
A gull cries derisively, in flight
its white turning black against the light.

from

Stoat, in Winter

Stoat, in Winter

Night filled my window.
Moving to curtain the dark
I saw, beyond the frame of light,
a stoat, winter-white
in my house-shadow.

Small head taut, it paused
alert at the lawn's edge,
seemingly passive, yet

extending slowly its seeking claws:
the kill imprinted in its eyes
old with inherited wisdoms
obedient to lore.

Sometimes now, when I see brides in white
I recall neither doves nor blossom
but that midwinter mammal in ermine,
its purity of commitment
to survival vows.

On Offa's Dyke

Once a concept, now returned to concept
except where the mounded soil
hints of activity, toil,
scoopings, bendings, craft
of earthwork unknit by wind-work.

Once a long snake, sinuous over the land,
over hill heights, above cwms:
now its disintegrated skin
is ghosted in the ground,
buried in its own earth
yet visible here and there
like the life of Offa, Mercian King.
This, in itself, evidence of him,
hegemony's power, fear —
                        the tangible remains.

Their truths the walls of history hold:
Hadrian's, Jerusalem's, Berlin's —
humanity walled in, walled out,
a wall for weeping on, a wall for execution;
and all our inner barriers, divisions
numerous as the species of wild growth
embedded in this dyke —
taken by the only natural army.

Llyn Brenig

(Man-made, 1976)

Where grouse rose cackling on the moor
and weasels sloped near farms
a new lake spreads like a water-fan
fringed with anchored fishermen.
Naked as a just-born child
surprised by its own existence
it lies self-consciously
skin wrinkling under the wind.

Birds are confused in migratory tracks.
On high ground, the cuffs of the forest
where uncountable sheep rush in eddies
woolly puppets on invisible wires
controlled by an unseen flockmaster.

The drowned valley knows again
the float of carboniferous seas
swish and hish of water-time
the sculpted art-work of ice.

Fox

Windblown sounds redouble, daub
the air. Single notes of horns
counterpoint collective baying,
invade all coverts, penetrate
each secret silence.

Outpacing his pursuers — hounds
of earth — the metaphysical fox
laughs in his heaven, as formless
he assumes another passing form.

I've seen him almost caught
trembling on a leaf-edge
or in a snatch of corn.
But always he eludes, transmutes
to this or that known shape. His earth
is everywhere.

I've glimpsed his flash
of tail-tip, circling
within circles in a field,
bringing his spiral course
to the hidden core.

Those pursuing hardest
in the tide of chase
often lose him first:
his scent evades —
submerged in water,
disguised in dung,
hiding among sheep,
pretending to be dead.
Is the pursuit ended?
Drowned in eternal silence?

No! Tally Ho again
this fox is up and sped.
The hounds are cast downwind.

from
Liverpool Folio

The Coming in of Ancestors

Here are the strangers with shabby holdalls
and pale enigmatic smiles:
they disembark, looking around uncertainly
as cloud-shadows move
on the moving Mersey;
and what they bring
is partly left at terminals;
and what they say
is scarcely comprehended.

Here are the docks, alive with arrivals,
cargoes of Irish, Germans, Poles.
Are they prepared
for what this land will give?
Will they, the foreigners,
ever feel they belong?
Perhaps not until their blood is passing
in the veins of English grandchildren.

My grandfather merges now
in the whisper of their lives:
his Scandinavian father
that whiskered man at chess
in the old, newly discovered photograph,
naturalised and with suitably altered name —
did he, as he slowly moved the chess pieces,
recall the forests, the fiords, the frozen winters?

My grandmother remembers her own:
Italian, in black toque hat,
wearing bright carnelian beads.

Here is their Liverpool —
the landfall in the west,
waterfront, heartland, home.

*A Liverpool Dock, 1982**

An empty sink.
No water, no ships.
A relief map of mud,
contours of ooze.
An opaque well.
Drop anything in here —
a ring, a boot, a body —
it will be stored without sign.

Memories too are sunk in there —
of cobbled quays with human throngs,
the clamour of cargoes, foreign tongues.
Above the mudline: 1849
the plaque's a reminder
everything falls
in the clogging hold
of time.

Pigeons and shadows inhabit warehouses,
weeds erupt through pavings,
bollards are fungus-furred.
And the river hurries by
preoccupied
with its own new silence.

*Prior to the regeneration of the Mersey docks as a heritage and leisure area

The Plaster Madonna

Spring in the streets brought conjecture
for the texture of flowers, known
only by their absence in that cemented world
where clouds, fleecing over from Wales,
held myths of scudding lamb and new-born bud.
I longed to have the scent of flowers,
to see and touch and know,
so resented the plaster madonna
of the virginal Catholic classroom
(May was proclaimed her month, blossom her prize).
The petalled offering at her feet
seemed pagan sacrifice to stiffest clay,
to dusty obscene toes, chipped carving,
faded paint and painted face
unable to see or touch or know
those flowers mine by right
of sight and yearning of the senses.

End of day, warm dust of May
moting the air, I stayed to evade
black moth nun along a corridor,
dark ghost in shafted sun
moving silently in childless school.
Disobeying the rule, child behind frosted glass
I hid, alone with the plaster madonna,
sinking in flower bliss, kissed
the smooth, incredible narcissi:
suspension of all
in the silent seeking senses.

Night-flitting nun (inevitably)
descended like a bat from Hades.
In spite of cloistered canticles and purity
of endless, incensed beads,
wrath uncensored rose from
those intensely dense medieval robes.

Outcast from the flowers, no fields
no dale, I ran renewed
through Everton Vale.

Ithaca-Liverpool

My father came today: an awaited visit,
the walk beachwards. Unusually quiet, he paced
the sand near the tide's persistent reach,
looking to the horizon broken by one dark ship.
'Like North Africa' he said suddenly. 'The war.
Thought I'd never return. I used to watch
from the shore, as from a desert island,
the convoys passing endlessly
carrying soldiers to who knows what.'
His eyes held the distance; in their deep grey
was a lost boy, an Odysseus never getting home.
When the war ended, his plane — approaching
English cliffs — turned back, defeated by fog;
like a great gull banking, it landed at Paris —
a city he never asked to know. Even now,
haunted in dreams, he sees them,
the ghost ships, passing silently, one by one.

Timepiece
(Liverpool Museum)

Those ebony clocks ticking velvet death
were chorus to every act in sable night,
circuiting the hours, dark and light,
like metronomes measuring breath.

I entered this gallery of time
at three on a winter afternoon
to a whirring, gonging, collective tune —
witnesses of the past utter the present chime —
ding-dong the daylong grief
tick-tock the gladness brief.

Some, like tall coffins stood on end,
with pale disc faces; a rare few
old water-clocks (what urgency then in mechanics new
to corner time flowing river-like round a bend?).

Others, in gold or silver filigree,
hold tiny jewelled mystery
made by the craftsman's hands, now gone,
while fingered time clicks on.

Time is life: we divide, watch, kill it.
Yet this, by Thomas Turner, 1788,
still sings an anthem of birth, death, fate
in the seconds of a minute.
Ding-dong the daylong grief
tick-tock the gladness brief.

Shop Window Models

Shop window models — stiff, elegant limbs,
taut lines, false hair, fixed faces —
when they are left lying sideways
on the floor in *rigor mortis,*
or stripped naked to reveal mock breasts,
attain a certain pathos, repel the eye
like the helpless sick in hospital beds
you walk past discreetly to the one you know.

On a Cobbler's Shelf

On a cobbler's shelf sit signs
of the struggle and surge of existence.
Styles and shapes yield significance,
suggest the mould of lives.

And those shoes preserved through the ages,
glass-cased and labelled —
thonged Roman sandals, leather like liquorice,
paste buckles of late rococo,
ice-skates worn by Wordsworth,
Charlotte Brontë's bird-thin slippers —
poignant portrayals of invisible wearers.

In a throw-away age, this Garston shop
is a survivor too, like its cobbler:
a pre-war craftsman, anecdotal,
gnarled, on the last.

The Pond, West Kirby Cliffs

The pond on the cliff has returned.
Through morning curtains I saw the gleam —
water catching the eastern light
clouds in a mirror in mud.
The pond has returned, and returning
mocks the machines, builders' outriders.

Wild the cliff, humpy the ground
a wasteland with ragged daisies,
the pond deep-centred, jagged.
That's how it was. Now the land's flattened
filled in, rolled out like lumpy pastry
ready for raw, rising structures.
I remember one swampy spring
when unaccustomed heat
vapoured the cliffs after rain,
the frogs rose in their masses,
simmered, leapt like court jesters,
overflowed the bacchanalian pond,
flopped round our gardens.
Many were squashed under car wheels,
burst like pods, flattened like cartoon cats
only to rise again to roundness
in the shape of countless kindred
whose eyes baled at dusk, thousands of them,
threatening the estate, ready to avenge,
throats pulsating, croaks uniting
in a twilight chorus.

The pond on the cliff has returned.
Not for long. A house will be cemented
over the place of springtime sex and spawning.
Concrete floors, foundations, walls.
But on moon-lost nights will an insideous croaking
be heard? And will a thousand bulging eyes
haunt the corners of the rooms?

From Hilbre Island

Dissolution of day
on the estuary;
night's vast advance
on the evening tide;
and I, rock-lichen, cling
listening to sea-distance,
the murmur of a harmony
within a greater harmony

while from the fretted shore
humanity emits
a thousand brutish sounds
diffused and lost:

as on a distant plain
the sound of centuries repeats
and noise of conflict boils
from blue-skinned warriors
or scaly knights who swarm
like early amphibians
floundering, sea-emerged.

from

Studies in Stone
'Not even the greatest artist has conceived an idea
a block of marble does not contain within itself.'
— Michelangelo, Sonnet 151 (*trans.* G. M. Coles)

Studies in Stone

Flint
tongues of varying lengths
blades without hafts

sharp slivers on a Clwyd hillside
sorted through, tossed away
only yesterday
by a small dark man
dressed in skins

Quartzite
durable enticement
of mica and crystal
sheep's skulls glittering with frost

fingers and fists, before Man,
knuckling above the highest ice

the Stiperstones, Devil-haunted

Jet
a necklace of lozenge beads
on white skin

Lenin's harbingers of death —
a line of black sledges
across the snow

Lapis Lazuli
curled in the eye of Horus
inlay of the sarcophagus

sparkle of pyrites
sun-flecks on a tideless sea

Eidyllion

The crags of Snowdon cry
    in creaking wind —
does Arthur sleep within?
    Bones of sheep
    whiten the cwms.

The rocks of Tryfan sigh
    in shrouding snow —
does Bedivere lie here?
    Ravens rise
    at Dinas Emrys.

And the waters of Llyn Llydaw
    whisper to the shore —
does Excalibur rest below?
    Samite fish
    hide in the rushes.

Rock Chapel, Clwydian Hills

(for Anna Haycraft)

Seen from the valley, impressive,
commanding, set high on a pulpit
of rock, grey finger admonishing the sky.
This little chapel gleams, beckons
like a Swiss scene.
I climb the lovers' path
through tilted trees. Thorns catch
from out the green.
Reaching the lip of cliff, I see
the living red — crimson fungi crushed
in its mossy bed. Outside, congregations
of leaves murmur their litanies. Inside

stillness, ancient silence. Only the motes —
particles of the past — move, dance an airy ritual.
On the altar, stiff oblation of dead flies,
legs fixed in supplication. I walk the aisle,
cleave the musty air. Stained glass, cracked,
casts a shadow-stigmata on off-white plaster.
Through sellotaped holes in the panes, sunlight
and spiders creep. A pieta droops in dust.

Lady of Sorrows for whom do you weep?
the human victim ever in your arms,
the bat-torn fieldmouse at your feet,
this, your deserted shrine?

Yet on bright mornings from the east
that daily benediction, sun — the world's host
in a monstrance of twigs — gilds
with pale light the fly-strewn altar,
the cobwebbed crucifix.

Castle Shapes, Clwydian Hills

If this is no castle of man
can it be simply mountain rock
wind-moulded, undevised?

If these are no constructed turrets
can they be purely nature's shape
pinnacles eroded, innocent
of power or terror's rape?

Then I am the flower
in the stone

the wisp of life
in a solid tomb-tower

obedient to experience
gracing this eternal fortress
with the pain of love

and a fragile death.

Winter in Clwyd: A Sequence

(for my mother, Gladys M. Reid)

1. Snow takes the mountains
   advance forces the frosts:
   no field escapes
   each blade sprigged
   like blast-dust on trees
   the fright-white ghosts of summer.
   The vale in frost-sprayed gown
   a thin hemline of mist
   below the hills.

2. The Clwydians' great white shoulders
   nude giants turned to stone
   hiding their faces.

3. A farmer's fence along the topmost field
   is a charcoal line demarcating
   from white hill the white sky.
   In the distance sheep move in flock —
   a yellow turgid river
   the dog fussing on its banks.

   Before me, pencilling of undergrowth
   pointillism of stubble. Closer now,
   I see bird-pricks, flick of wings,
   fox-marks narrow with long central toes,
   indentations of dragged tails — rats
   or slender weasels — the matchless blobs
   of rabbits and, behind, unmistakable
   manprints. Secretly in snow
   new graphics have appeared.

4. Light breaks over eastern Clwyd:
   the hill hollows fill like breakfast bowls
   milky to the brim. Snow on the tops,
   crystalline mounds dissolving
   at the edge. Changing light eludes
   no matter how long I stare.
   I notice how mountains, their fronts
   in deep pleats at early morning
   become smoothed out by coffee-time.
   I hold a steaming mug: froth clings
   like stale snow the rain disperses.

5. On the chess board of fields
   a dark King stands cornered
   in check to a white Queen:
   the heavy oak, immobile, hedged in
   before a silver birch, slim
   moving in all directions.
   It's the wind's game.

N44, France: Holiday Route

Maize, wheat, vines border the road,
a straight road, one hour to Rheims,
this the country of Champagne.
The celebration wine from sad flatlands;
white of the white grape
from a blood-soaked earth.
Signposts are to cemeteries,
graves, as neat and thickly planted
as the rows of vines. No bubbles here,
no sparkle. On one side a crucifix;
on the other, a stone hand holding
a stone flame. A little stone for every man.
War is soil-deep here, though the maize
grows fine ears, the vines have luscious grapes —
all this ground seems tender,
vulnerable. Hardly breathing, not believing
in any harvest, least of all its own.

Yes, there are poppies, still in abundance;
neither are the larks absent, nor their singing.
Yet the peace now lying over this landscape
seems merely a transfer about to be peeled back
to reveal the real scene: battle, ambush.
Trees seem about to explode;
fields, copses, grassy knolls
all units in the strategy, the campaign.

While Mephistopheles drinks champagne
an angel smiles through centuries of war
over the cathedral door
at Rheims, where hotels offer the best of wine
and tourists stay, less to mourn than dine.

Michelangelo's David

In this stone colossus
is there a resemblance
to the nimble boy
messiah-fated to kill a giant
with one blow? Did he
(in life larger than life)
look keen in sculpted grace
brood in sinewed strength
fix thought in frozen frown?
And were his mobile eyes
as marble-steady; was he
ready with his sling?

When Goliath faced the boy
did he see a small statue,
glimpse the sudden stone
of death?

This David is a stone Goliath.

At Haworth

Roots of cloudberry
among the nardus grass.
Gritstone for grinding
is lion shapes in the crags.
Walls shift and settle
as the moorland moves.

The gravestones sag,
battalions of them;
and the fortress line
of linked cottages
fronts horizontal wind,
diagonal rain.

No wonder the cobbles
huddle together
and flat slabs shield
those beds of the dead.
Yet there are times when
the Parsonage glows
like topaz.

My Jade King

You stand at the centre of my room.
Each day I admire your texture —
smooth, glossy almost.
Your contours catch me, carved
to my pleasure. You never fail
in aesthetic appeal. Yet sometimes
you reveal your subtle hidden green,
show an alien aspect, smile turned
to snarl. An inward change, not caused
by sinister light or the day's mood.
But then, you have the qualities of jade —
green veined in varying shades,
comparative softness yet sound self-structure:
even if I drop you, you won't smash.

Of jade's five properties, two are yours,
those most appropriate to a king:
courage, certainly; a degree of wisdom.
And the legendary healing power of jade?
precious to Aztecs as 'stone of the loin',
prescribed by early physicians
to be taken internally (though a dose
is fatal). Yes, I know you can cure:
successfully cauterising my naive belief,
antidote to chronic 'in love'.
Indispensable. Always I will want you
on my shelf.

Gargoyles

Stone on stone devoid of bone.
Granule hearts. All solid parts.
Everything externalised. Grotesques
always in the beautiful high places.
One time (not long ago) those faces
spilling expression, spouting thought
invariably caught me in wart-caress,
clutched inner gargoyles, clawed my water-images.

Now I'm gauging fear, its forms, the chimera:
seeing, last summer, the famed four of Paris
fixed in surveillance on Notre Dame —
Thinker out-thinking thought, Dragon
all arched ferocity, grape-grasping Eagle
and that eternal, entirely expected
Devil (ridiculously griffin, almost pet).
These no longer startle. Familiar, chromatic
on postcards sent to Illinois or Marple.
Tourist appeal like Auschwitz, Anne Frank's house
the Bloody Tower or other of life's gibbets.

Unexpected ones still knife me:
reptile boughs in meres,
rock beasts with glaring fossil eyes,
dark, omnipresent Satans in the sky.